Man and God

A Bible Study on the Most Valuable Thing in Your Life

KOREA NAVPRESS
To know Christ and to make Him known

The Navigators is an international, evangelical Christian organization. Jesus Christ gave his followers the Great Commission in Matthew 28:19: "Go therefore and make disciples of all nations." The primary aim of The Navigators is to help fulfill that commission by multiplying laborers for Jesus Christ in every nation.

Korea NavPress is the publishing ministry of The Korean Navigators. Korea NavPress publishes books and materials for the spiritual growth of Christians. We help believers become committed disciples of Jesus Christ and become laborers who have mature character and leadership.

CONTENTS

What is your destination?

Our life is like a trip on a train. What is the final destination of this trip? Where do we come from and where are we going?

Today, this is still a difficult question to many people. But there is one who said, "I know where I come from and where I am going." Do you know who he is? He is Jesus Christ. He said, "I came from the Father and entered the world; now I am leaving the world and going back to the Father"(John 16:28).

Do you know, then, where you come from and where you are going?

This booklet is designed to help you answer to the above question. You can study this booklet by yourself, but you are encouraged to do this Bible study in a group with others. You will find, then, that sharing your answers with others in a group will aid and deepen your understanding. To do this Bible study, you must search the Bible and prepare an answer to each of the questions in this study booklet before you come to the group. Be ready to share and discuss your answers.

Continue to study this material without exception over 5 weeks with a sincere and serious attitude. Then you can certainly find satisfying answer to the above question.

The five lessons in this booklet are:

- God's Concerns
- Man's Condition
- God's Solution
- Man's Responsibility
- New Life in Jesus Christ

▶ For those who do not have the Old Testament,
Old Testament verses are listed at the end of each chapter.

Lesson 1

God's Concerns

God's Plan for Man

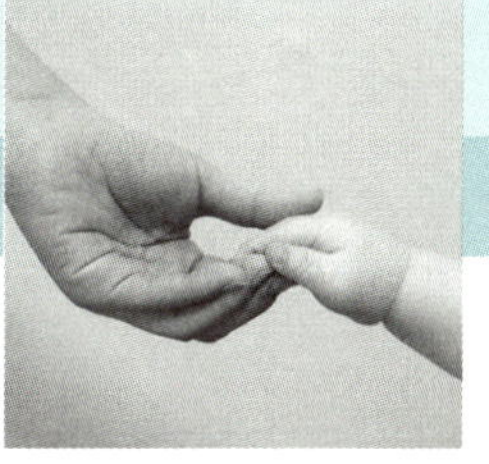

Everything that exists in this world has its own meaning and purpose. Even a matchstick is not made without any meaning but made with a clear purpose. What, then, is the meaning and purpose of our lives?

1. In Genesis 1:27, God created man "in his own image." Why do you think God made man "in his own image"?

2. What is God's purpose in calling us? (I Corinthians 1:9)

3. What did Jesus say about his purpose in coming into this world? (John 10:10)

The Bible says that man is God's creation. God created man in his own image in order to have loving fellowship with man. Jesus also came into the world in order to give us new life so that we can have fellowship with God and live an abundant life. God is still calling us to have fellowship with him today.

Our Life (Our Condition)

4. What do you think is an “abundant life”?

5. What do you think is the reason that many people do not live the abundant life which God designed for us?

6. Are you living an abundant life now?

Everyone longs to live an abundant life. They hear that happiness is just over the next hill, so they do their best to climb the hill in order to achieve happiness. However, they find that happiness is yet again just over the next hill. Man has an innate desire to pursue happiness. Yet, if man does not understand his own condition, this pursuit of happiness can prove elusive and frustrating.

In the next lesson we will discover what the Bible says about the condition of man.

▶ For those who do not have the Old Testament:

Genesis 1:27 God created man in his own image, in the image of God he created him; male and female he created them.

Lesson 2

MAN'S CONDITION

The Bible says, "We all, like sheep, have gone astray, each of us has turned to his own way"(Isaiah 53:6).

Why are we compared to sheep? Sheep cannot survive without a shepherd. Sheep tend to go their own way, not knowing whether their way leads to a barren land, or to a steep cliff, or to a lion waiting for its prey. We also have these sheep-like characteristics.

All Have Sinned

1. In Psalm 14:1-3, what does the author say about the people who tend to go their own way?

2. In the following verses, what is the description of sin?

Isaiah 53:6

Jeremiah 2:13

3. Who has sinned? (Romans 3:23)

What is the result of sin? (Isaiah 59:2)

4. The Bible says, "All have sinned." Do you think that you are included in the "All"?

Sin not only separates us from God, but also makes us enemies of God. A dreadful penalty for sin is waiting for us. God is so holy and righteous that he never overlooks our sin.

The Unavoidable Penalty for Sin

5. What is the result of our sin?
   Hebrews 9:27

   Revelation 21:8

Man makes a great effort to solve the problem which sin causes. For example, man tries to solve it by good deeds, religious activities, education, philosophy, and righteous living. However, none of these can save us from the result of sin, nor lead us to true happiness which we seek.

Cannot Be Saved by Our Own Efforts

6. What do the following verses say?
   Ephesians 2:8-9

   John 6:28-29

   Galatians 2:16

   I Corinthians 1:21

   Acts 4:12

7. Do you think that there is any way for us to save ourselves by our own efforts?

8. Review this lesson. What have you learned?

▶ For those who do not have the Old Testament:

Psalms 14:1-3	The fool says in his heart, "There is no God." They are corrupt, their deeds are vile; there is no one who does good. The Lord looks down from heaven on the sons of men to see if there are any who understand, any who seek God. All have turned aside, they have together become corrupt; there is no one who does good, not even one.
Isaiah 53:6	We all, like sheep, have gone astray, each of us has turned to his own way; and the Lord has laid on him the iniquity of us all.
Jeremiah 2:13	My people have committed two sins: They have forsaken me, the spring of living water, and have dug their own cisterns, broken cisterns that cannot hold water.
Isaiah 59:2	But your iniquities have separated you from your God; your sins have hidden his face from you, so that he will not hear.

Lesson 3

GOD'S SOLUTION

God did not abandon us who were perishing through a sinful life. He took the initiative to solve our problems. When we were still sinners, God demonstrated his love for us by making the way to salvation at the cross.

God's Love

1. How did God show his love? (John 3:16)

What does “the world” and “his one and only Son” mean respectively?

2. While we were still sinners, what happened to us? (Romans 5:8)

What is the reason that Christ died? (I John 4:10)

Christ Received the Penalty for Our Sin

3. What is another reason that Christ died? (Refer to Romans 6:23 and I Peter 2:24)

4. What kind of grace did we receive as a result of Christ's death on the cross?

I Peter 3:18

II Corinthians 5:18

5. What did John the Baptist say when he met Jesus Christ? (John 1:29)

The cross was originally used as a tool of execution for a death sentence. It was made of wood and the criminal was fastened by ropes and nailed down to it. In order to receive the penalty for sin in our place, Jesus Christ died on the same cross that was used as a method of execution. Through the death of Christ on the cross, God broke the barrier of sin that separated us from God and made the bridge for salvation through which everyone can come to God by faith.

6. The more wonderful fact recorded in the Bible is that Jesus Christ not only died for our sins but also ______________________ ______________________. (I Corinthians 15:3-4)

7. What does Jesus' resurrection show about who he is? (Romans 1:4)

8. What does it mean to you that Jesus Christ died for our sins and rose again from the dead?

9. What is the final destiny for those who believe in Jesus and those who do not? (John 3:36)

▶ Gospel is...

Gospel is the good news that according to the Scriptures Jesus Christ died for our sins, was buried, and was raised on the third day.

Lesson 4

MAN'S RESPONSIBILITY

God made the bridge to salvation, 'the cross', to save us from sin and eternal death. However, it is of no use if we do not cross the bridge. Jesus said, "I am the way and the truth and the life. No one comes to the Father except through me"(John 14:6). It is our responsibility to come to God through the way to salvation, Jesus Christ.

Choice by Faith

1. Two different ways have been set before us. What are they? (John 3:18)

Who should make this choice?

2. What does John 3:16 say we must do to get eternal life instead of eternal condemnation?

3. What blessings are promised to those who hear Jesus' word and believe? (John 5:24)

4. What is the will of God for those who do not believe? (John 6:40)

Believe = Receive

5. What does it mean to believe in Jesus? (John 1:12)

6. Read Revelations 3:20.

(1) Who is knocking at the door? Whose door is it?

(2) Why is he knocking at the door?

(3) What does it mean to open the door?

To believe in Jesus Christ means to receive him as one's Savior and Lord.

7. How can we receive Jesus Christ into our heart? (Romans 10:9-10)

We can receive Jesus Christ into our heart by praying as follows:

"Lord, I acknowledge that I am a sinner. I believe that Jesus Christ died on the cross for my sins and rose from the dead. Now I want to receive Jesus Christ into my life as my personal Savior and Lord. Please come into my heart and lead my life. I pray in Jesus' name. Amen."

8. Did you receive Jesus Christ wholeheartedly?

Then where is Jesus Christ now?

How do you know it?

Memorize I John 5:11-12 for your assurance of salvation.

"And this is the testimony: God has given us eternal life, and this life is in his Son. He who has the Son has life; he who does not have the Son of God does not have life."

Lesson 5

NEW LIFE IN JESUS CHRIST

The following is the summary of what we have studied up to now.

- God wants us to live an abundant life through loving fellowship with him.
- All men have sinned, and as a result have gone astray from God, the origin of life. Without God, man cannot live an abundant life, and will be condemned to death.
- Our God, who loves us, sent Jesus Christ to this world, and made him the bridge to salvation through his death on the cross by laying our sin's penalty on him.
- Anyone who hears the gospel and crosses the bridge by faith—that is, whoever receives Jesus Christ—will not perish but have eternal life.

Assurance of Salvation

1. On what basis are we able to have the assurance of salvation?
   I John 5:13

   John 20:31

2. The following verses are about salvation. Summarize the key contents of each verse.
   Ephesians 2:8-9

   I Peter 1:23

Romans 10:13

John 10:28-29

John 1:12

Hebrews 10:17

3. Are you sure that you are saved? How can you know it?

We can have the assurance of salvation by believing God's promises recorded in the Bible. Our feelings and emotions cannot be the basis of our assurance of salvation. We need to be assured of our salvation according to the promises which God gave us in the Bible, not our feelings and emotions, which can change anytime.

Enjoy Salvation

4. What do the following verses say about the new life of a Christian?
   II Corinthians 5:17

   Galatians 2:20

5. What do the following verses say about the blessings which the saved receive as children of God?
   John 16:24

I Corinthians 10:13

I John 1:9

Proverbs 3:5-6

It is hardly possible to explain all the blessings which we can enjoy as children of God in this simple booklet. However, we can find and enjoy these wonderful blessings when we regularly study the Bible that God gave us as spiritual food, and we can grow up healthily in the spiritual life.

▶ For those who do not have the Old Testament:

Proverbs 3:5-6 Trust in the Lord with all your heart and lean not on your own understanding; in all your ways acknowledge him, and he will make your paths straight.

Now you have become a Christian.

This is great news. You, as a child of God, now have the great privilege to enjoy all the blessings that God has promised. In the Bible, there are so many promises that God gives us and all of them are like jewels. You can find and possess the jewels when you continue to read, study, memorize, and meditate on God's word.

> "And if you look for it as for silver and search for it as for hidden treasure, then you will understand the fear of the Lord and find the knowledge of God"(Proverbs 2:4-5).

In addition, you must grow spiritually. If you received Jesus Christ and became a child of God, you have been born again as a spiritual infant. The birth of a new life is a great blessing and joy. However, if the newborn child does not grow, it would create great anxiety instead of great joy. Therefore you must grow spiritually. As a baby is nourished by his or her mother's milk, a newborn Christian also needs to take God's word, which is spiritual nutrition. Enjoy the great joy of spiritual growth by taking God's word regularly.

Man and God

Korea NavPress
16 Yeonhuiro, Sudaemungu, Seoul 03784
http://navpress.co.kr

ISBN 978-89-375-0459-4 03230

First printing, 2014
Second printing, 2021

Printed in Korea